Hans-Günter Heumann

Piano Junior

A Creative and Interactive
Piano Course for Children

Lesson Book 1

ED 13801

Illustrations by Leopé

SCHOTT

Mainz · London · Berlin · Madrid · New York · Paris · Prague · Tokyo · Toronto

ED 13801
British Library Cataloguing-in-Publication Data.
A catalogue record for this book is available from the British Library
ISMN 979-0-2201-3635-1
ISBN 978-1-84761-425-4

English translation: Schott London Editorial
Design and typesetting by www.bbruemmer.de
Illustration on page 10 by Elke Göpfert
Stockphotos: Icons (Playing Corner, Composing Corner)
Cover design: www.adamhaystudio.com
Music setting: Darius-Heise-Krzyszton
Audio tracks recorded, mixed and mastered by Clements Pianos
Audio tracks performed by Samantha Ward and Maciej Raginia
Videos produced by Ben Tillett
Printed in Germany S&Co. 9200

About the Author

Hans-Günter Heumann is a freelance composer and author, living in southern Germany.

Since studying piano, composition, and music pedagogy at the Musikhochschule Hannover, followed by further studies in the USA, he has dedicated himself to the editing of pedagogical piano material. He has a particular interest in presenting music in an accessible way to reach a broad audience.

Based on many years of experience teaching children, young people and adults, Hans-Günter has written a great number of internationally successful and award winning publications, and has composed and arranged piano music in a range of styles for beginners to advanced students.

Having developed successful, methodical concepts for learning how to play the piano for all age groups and abilities, Hans-Günter's work has been translated into many different languages and sold millions of copies, an indication of the wide-spread appreciation of his work.
His publications *Klavierspielen – mein schönstes Hobby* and *Piano Kids* (both published by Schott Music) have become two of the most significant piano methods in the German language.

Acknowledgments

The author and publishers would like to thank Prof. Carolyn True, Melanie Spanswick and Dr. Sally Cathcart for expert suggestions, support and advice in the development of *Piano Junior*.

Introduction

Piano Junior is a creative and interactive piano course for children from the age of 6, which progresses in small, manageable steps. It is a fun and satisfying approach to playing and learning about music, encouraging quick and noticeable progress.

Piano Junior is home to PJ, a robot with great enthusiasm for the piano, who accompanies and motivates children throughout the piano course. On PJ's homepage **www.piano-junior.com** you will find a video introduction and demonstrations, audio tracks of all pieces played on an acoustic piano, further fun practice resources and other interactive elements.

This innovative course stimulates and encourages creativity through regular, integrated 'Corners', such as *Composing, Improvising, Action, Playing, Technique, Ear Training, Memory, Sight-Reading* and *Music Quizzes*. In this way solid musical knowledge and technical ability is acquired. The experience of learning the piano is multifaceted: aural – with regular ear-training exercises; visual – with sight-reading; tactile – with clear explanations of technical aspects of playing and, above all, creative – with exercises in composing and improvising.

The choice of pieces includes attractive works from the classical period to the present day as well as interesting arrangements of folk tunes and children's songs, classical masterpieces, jazz and pop melodies.

In addition to the **Lesson Book** (which includes Exercises) at each level there is also: a **Theory Book**, in which valuable information from the method is worked through and consolidated in a playful, imaginative way. There is also a **Duet Book** at each level, to provide motivation for playing the piano with others and a **Performance Book** with great repertoire, which is fun to play. The *Flash Cards* included can be used to provide further practice in note reading, with musical symbols/terms and with rhythm patterns. By collecting the cards from each volume you will acquire a wealth of reference material.

Music greatly enriches the life of a child and **Piano Junior** aims to provide a musical basis for this in the most creative and motivating way.

Hans-Günter Heumann

 Theory Book

 Duet Book

 Performance Book

Reference to material at
www.piano-junior.com:

▶ Video **1** | Audio Track **1** | Rhythm Check **1** |
Workout **1** | Sight-Reading **1**

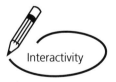
Interactivity

Contents

Flash Cards 1 (inserts): Notes, Musical Symbols / Terms, Rhythm

Hello!

I am Piano Junior, or PJ to my friends! I am a little robot and absolutely love playing the piano.
I really want to show you everything about the piano and how to play it. I'd like to be your friend and helper.
You can find out more about me in my profile. I have left space for you to fill in your own profile next to mine.

PJ's Profile

Name: Piano Junior, 'PJ' for short

Who I am: I am a robot with very flexible arms and hands, as well as lots of other special features. Everything we learn together is stored in my virtual brain.

Things I like: Music!!! Especially the piano ☺

Things I don't like: Tests at school, tidying my room, oiling my joints, and recharging my battery ☹

My best friend: Mozart, my little dog, named after the famous composer Wolfgang Amadeus Mozart

My hobbies: Playing the piano, listening to and dreaming about music, and dancing

What I like doing: Playing the piano with friends and sharing my favourite music

...............'s Profile

Name: ....

Who I am: ....

....

....

Things I like: ....

Things I don't like: ....

....

My best friend: ....

My hobbies: ....

....

What I like doing: ....

....

www.piano-junior.com

In all the books you will find this sign: ▶ This means you can visit my homepage. There are lots of things to discover.

Watching   Watch video tutorials for some of the pieces in this book.

Listening   You can hear all the pieces and exercises played on a piano.

Download   Download extra, fun material to help you improve

Here We Go!

I hope you have lots of fun and great success in learning to play the piano with me.

Good luck!
PJ

UNIT 1: The Piano

How the Piano Works

Each key on the piano produces a different note. All the keys together are called a keyboard. When you press a key down, a small felt hammer inside the instrument hits a steel string and makes it sound. This produces a note. There is one hammer for every note on the keyboard.

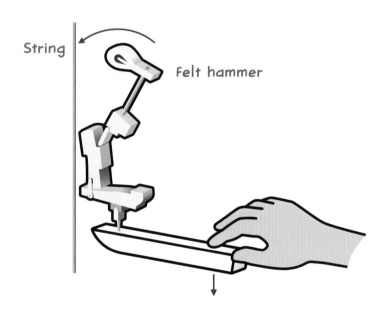

String

Felt hammer

Strings

Felt hammers

Keyboard

Pedals

How to Sit at the Piano

Sit in an upright but relaxed position at the centre of the keyboard. Your fingers should touch the keys so that your forearm, wrist and back of your hand form a straight line. You can adjust the height of the piano stool to be comfortable.

Position of the Arms and Hands

To relax the arms and hands, first let them hang at your sides in a natural way, as if you were walking. Then place your hands in this position on the keyboard.

Hand and Finger Position

Your fingers should be gently curved, making a bridge with your knuckles. Only your fingertips should touch the keys; your thumb should be slightly curved too.

Water Drop Point

Imagine the point at which a drop of water drips from the end of your finger. Your finger should touch the key in a similar way.

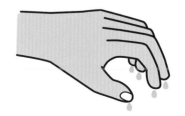

➡ Place your hands, palms together, vertically in front of you (see picture 1).

➡ Open your hands to form a gently curved shape (2).

➡ Open and close each pair of fingers, one after another, beginning with the thumbs, then the index fingers, and so on (3). The fingers should touch at the water drop points.

T1
page 8/9

When playing the piano, each finger is given a number. These numbers appear above or below the notes, showing which fingers to play the notes with. The numbers are known as **fingering** and should always be followed.

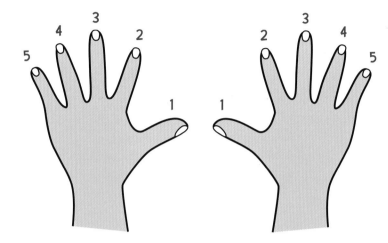

Finger Games

1.

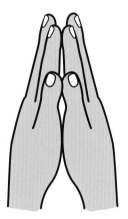

2.

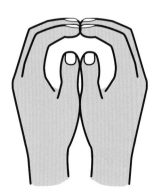

3.

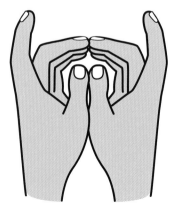

UNIT 2: The Keyboard
page 10/11

The complete collection of piano keys is called the **keyboard**, made up of white and black keys. Each key produces a different note. The piano keyboard usually has 88 keys.

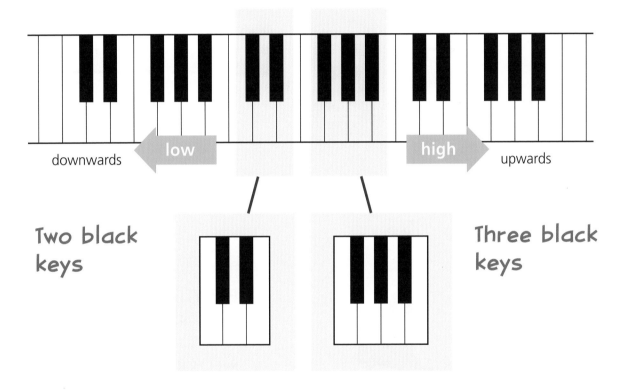

downwards | low | high | upwards

Two black keys

Three black keys

The black keys are arranged in groups of two and three, which can help you to find your way around the keyboard.

PLAYING CORNER

➡ Choose a group of two black keys and the group of three black keys next to it. Play these with the third finger of the right hand, upwards and downwards.

➡ Also do this with the left hand.

➡ These five notes sound really good with the pedal. Try this out. Press the right pedal down with the right foot and then play the groups of two and three notes.

➡ Can you think of a nice melody? Have a go! Combine the five notes in different orders. You can also repeat notes if you like.

Kangaroo Hop

Two Black Keys

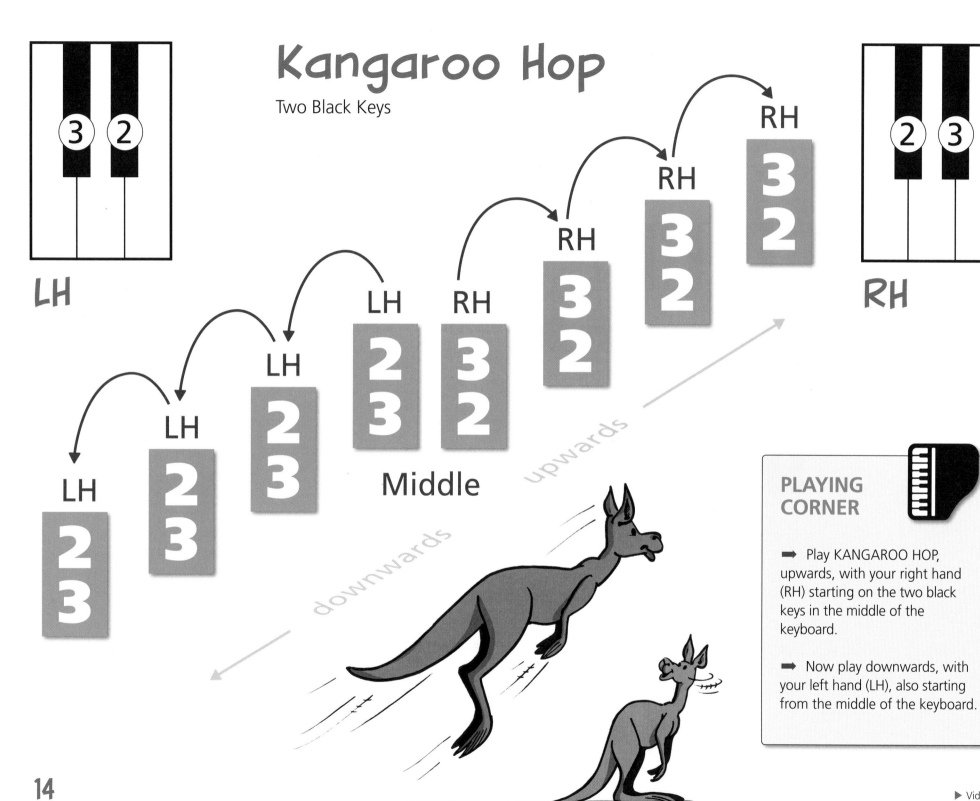

Middle

downwards

upwards

PLAYING CORNER

➡ Play KANGAROO HOP, upwards, with your right hand (RH) starting on the two black keys in the middle of the keyboard.

➡ Now play downwards, with your left hand (LH), also starting from the middle of the keyboard.

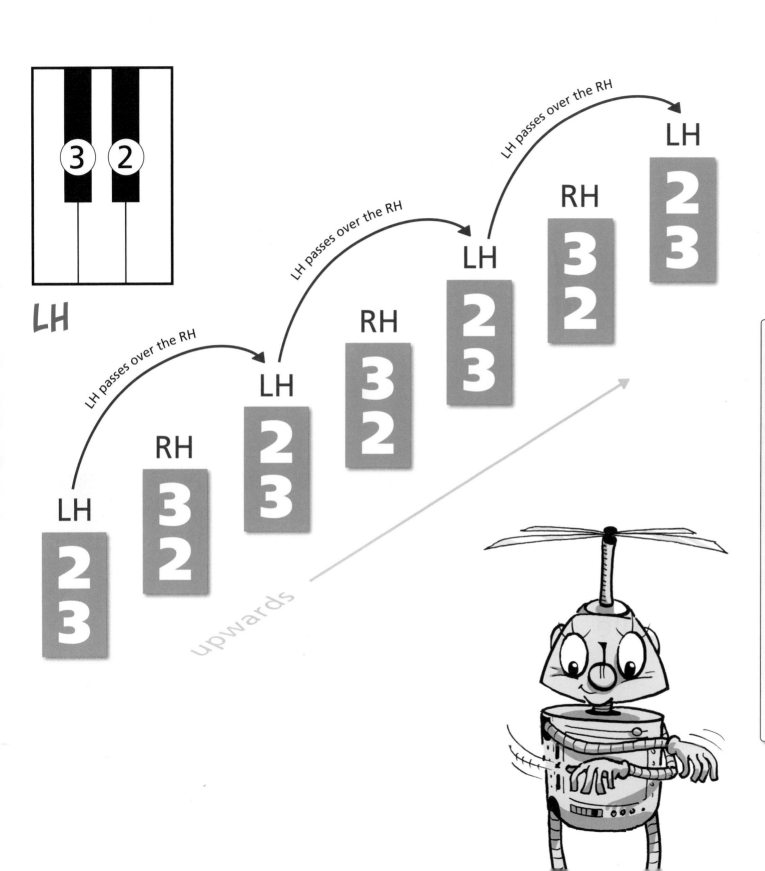

LH

3 2

RH

2 3

LH passes over the RH

LH passes over the RH

LH passes over the RH

LH
2
3

RH
3
2

LH
2
3

RH
3
2

LH
2
3

RH
3
2

LH
2
3

upwards

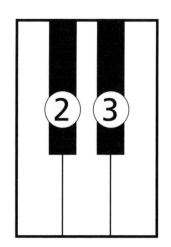

RH

2 3

PLAYING CORNER

➡ Play the groups of two black keys over the whole keyboard. Begin with the lowest group of two in the LH, then play the next group with the RH. Now the LH passes over the RH, then the RH moves to the next group, and so on.

➡ When you reach the highest notes, you can begin to play the same pattern down the keyboard. This time, begin with the RH, followed by the LH. The RH then passes over the LH, then the LH moves to the next group, and so on.

15

Kangaroo Hop

Three Black Keys

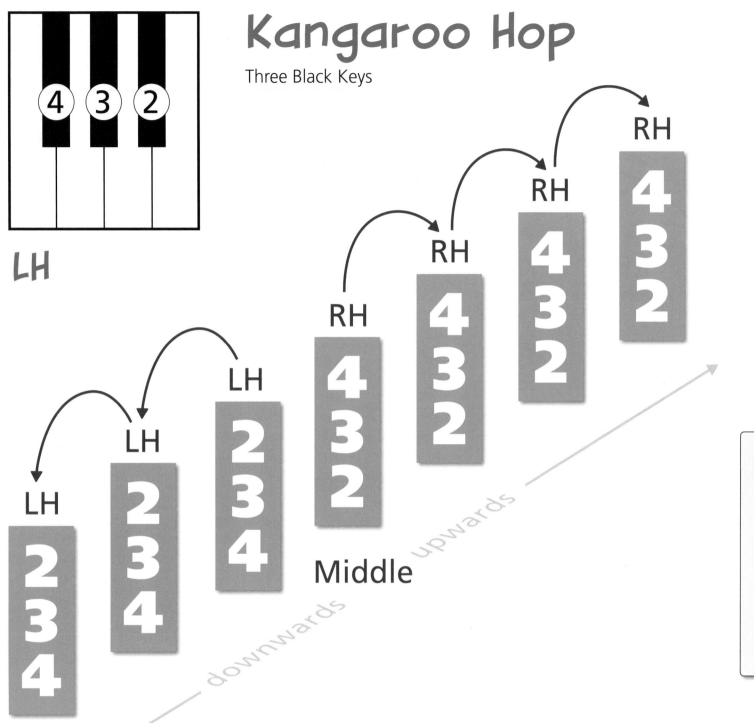

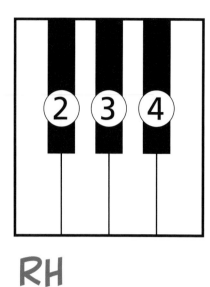

PLAYING CORNER

➡ Play KANGAROO HOP with your RH from the middle of the keyboard upwards.

➡ Now play with your LH from the middle of the keyboard downwards.

▶ Video **2**

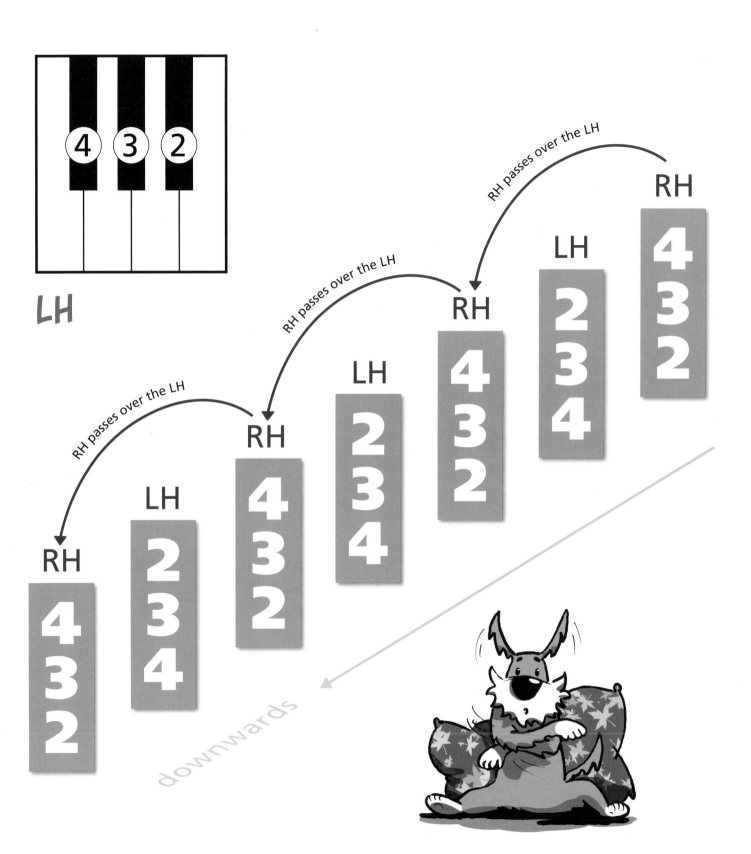

LH

RH passes over the LH

RH passes over the LH

RH passes over the LH

downwards

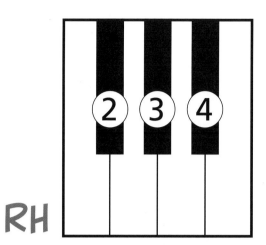

RH

➡ Play the groups of three black notes over the whole keyboard. Begin with the highest group of three in the RH, then play the next group of three with the LH. Now the RH passes over the LH, then the LH moves to the next group, and so on.

➡ When you reach the lowest notes, you can play the same pattern up the keyboard. This time begin with the LH, followed by the RH. The LH then passes over the RH, then the RH moves to the next group, and so on.

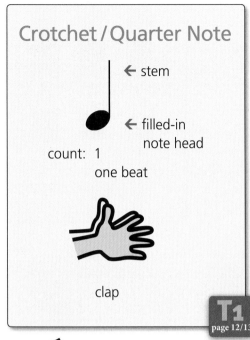

← stem

← filled-in note head

count: 1

one beat

clap

T1
page 12/13

ACTION CORNER

➡ While your teacher plays the piece BOOGIE BEAT, you clap the beat in time. Your teacher will play it slowly first, then at a faster tempo.

➡ Now walk in time to the music, either around the room or on the spot, again first at a slow tempo, then faster. Make sure you step in time with the music.

Unit 3:
The Beat in Music

Music usually has a regular beat, or pulse, similar to the beating of the heart.

The beat or pulse can have different **tempos** – from very slow to very fast.

Boogie Beat

Accompaniment

HGH

♩ = 60 + 144

sim.

f *L. H. marcato*   *sim.*

© 2016 Schott Music Limited, London

Boogie Beat

RH

This row x 8

This row x 1

This row x 3

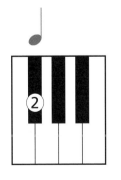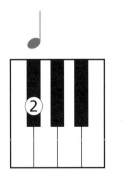

PLAYING CORNER

➡ Play BOOGIE BEAT with your teacher.
Play the first row eight times, the second row just once and the third row three times. Always try to hear and feel the beat. Have fun playing together!

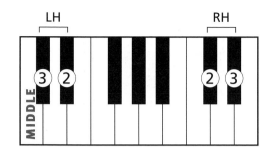

Duck Walk

HGH

RH

Wad-dle, wad-dle,   quack, quack, quack, quack, it's so fun-ny, wad-dle, quack, quack.

LH

count: **1**

Final Bar Line

The end of a piece is indicated by a double bar line, made up of two lines: a thin one, followed by a thick one.

Accompaniment

♩ = 60

mf

Tick Tock Clock

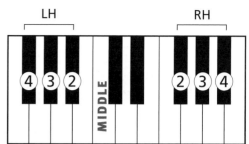

RH

2 3 4   2

Clocks go tick tock   tick tock, tick tock, clocks will ne - ver go to bed.

LH

4 3 2   4

count: 1 – 2

= ♩ + ♩

HGH

Minim / Half Note T1
page 14/15

← stem

← clear note head

count: 1 – 2
two beats

clap hold

PLAYING CORNER

Play the notes in this piece short and detached. Imitate the sound of your teacher by listening.

Accompaniment

♩ = 60

mf

Camel Ride

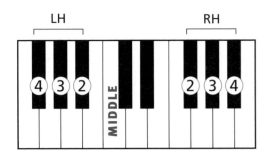

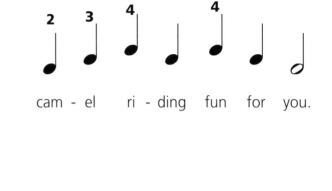

HGH

RH

Cam - el ride at the zoo, cam - el ri - ding fun for you.

LH

legato

legato

Play smoothly, without gaps between the notes.
Keep the legato effect as the melody passes from one hand to the other. Begin playing legato with a downwards movement of the arm and end with an upwards movement of the wrist.

Repeat Sign

The repeat sign is similar to the double bar line at the end of a piece, but also has two dots. It means play again from the beginning.

Accompaniment

Mary Had a Little Lamb

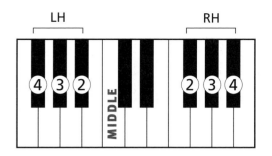

English Nursery Rhyme

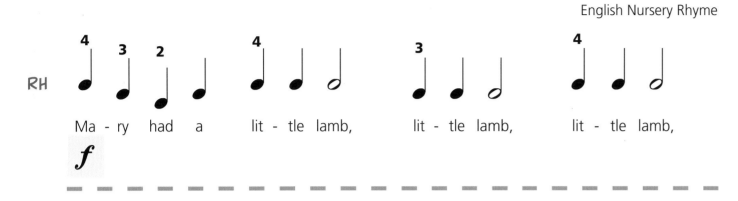

RH

Ma - ry had a   lit - tle lamb,   lit - tle lamb,   lit - tle lamb,

f

LH

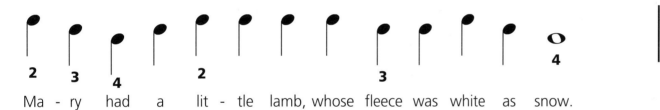

Ma - ry had a   lit - tle lamb, whose fleece was white as snow.

Accompaniment

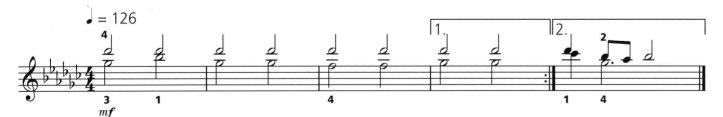

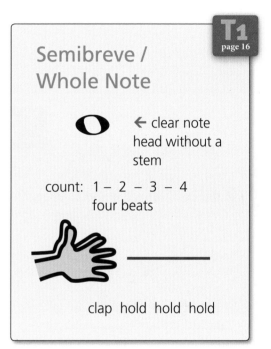

T1 page 16

Semibreve / Whole Note

○ ← clear note head without a stem

count: 1 – 2 – 3 – 4
four beats

clap hold hold hold

Dynamics

f **forte** = loud

The term **Dynamics** means the different levels of volume in a piece. These differences make music more expressive.

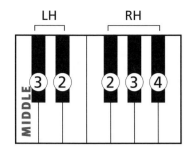

p **piano** = soft

T1 page 17

The Bar/Measure

Each melody is divided into bars. A bar contains a number of beats which are grouped by bar lines.

bar line

bar   bar

Always emphasize the note after the bar line.

Sad Clown

HGH

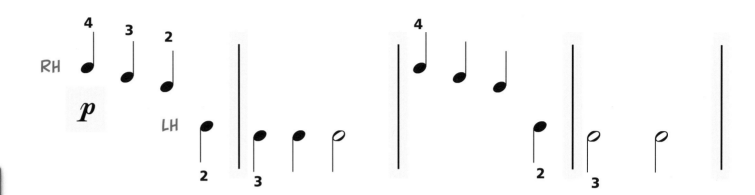

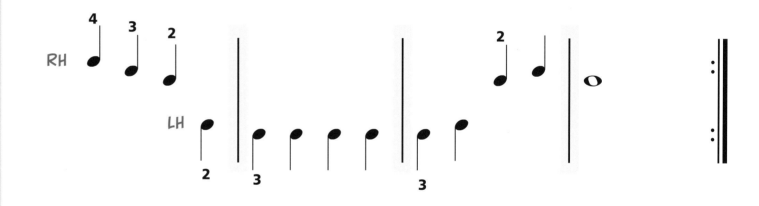

Accompaniment

© 2016 Schott Music Limited, London

Old MacDonald Had a Farm

Children's Song from the USA

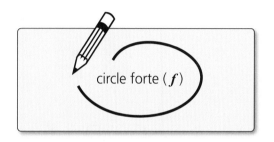

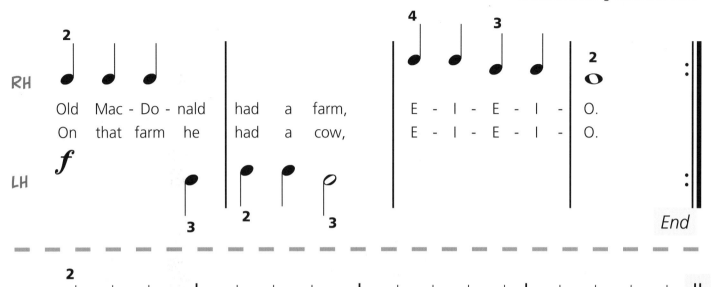

RH

Old Mac - Do - nald had a farm, E - I - E - I - O.
On that farm he had a cow, E - I - E - I - O.

f

LH

End

RH

Moo, Moo, here, moo, moo, there, here a moo, moo, there a moo, moo.

Back to the beginning

circle forte (*f*)

A double bar line divides a piece of music into sections.

Accompaniment With Accompaniment, student plays one octave higher than written.

♩ = 88

f

Fine

D. C. al Fine

▶ Video **9** | Audio Track **13/14**

25

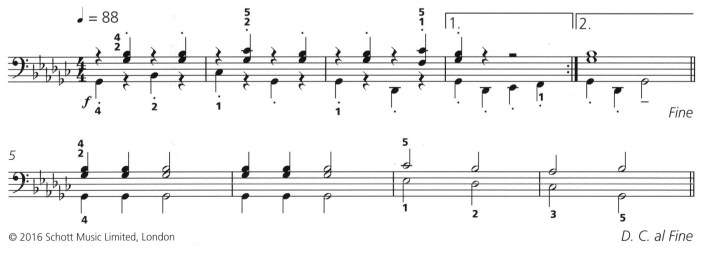

UNIT 4: The White Keys T1 page 18
Three White Keys C-D-E

C D E

The notes C-D-E form a group around the two black keys, and are repeated several times over the keyboard. The groups of two black notes help you to find them.

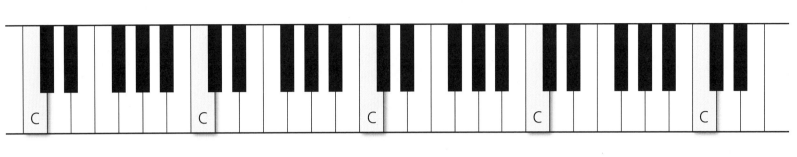

C

 lies to the left of the group of two black notes

D

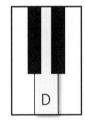 lies between two black notes

E

 lies to the right of the group of two black notes

PLAYING CORNER

Play the notes C-D-E, in any order. Play them on low and high notes.

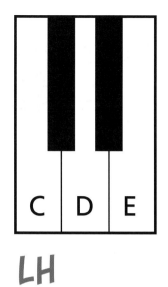

LH

Fly a Kite

Three White Keys

RH

PLAYING CORNER

➡ Play FLY A KITE starting on the lowest C on the piano.

➡ Now play the piece beginning on the next highest C upwards, and so on.

LH passes over the RH

28

Haunted House

Black and White Keys

circle piano (*p*)

HGH

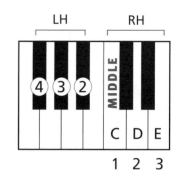

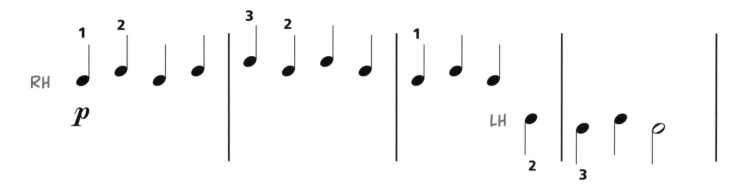

Accompaniment

♩ = 69

UNIT 5: The 5-Finger Position

5 White Keys C – D – E – F – G

C Position

Put the thumb of your RH on C.
The other fingers rest on the neighbouring white notes.
This is the 5-finger position. The lowest note in each hand gives the name of the position.

If you place each finger of your hands on neighbouring white notes, your hands will be in a close five-finger position. Keep your fingers in this position for the whole piece.

G

F

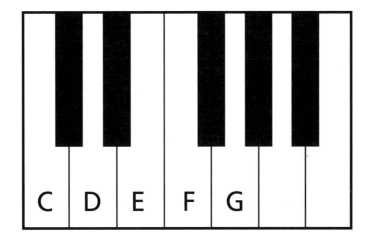

C D E F G

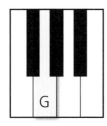

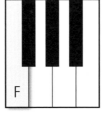

F

lies to the left of the group of three black notes

G

lies between the first and second of the group of three black notes

▶ Workout 5

5-Finger Fun

HGH

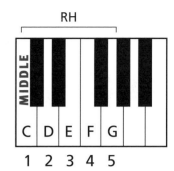

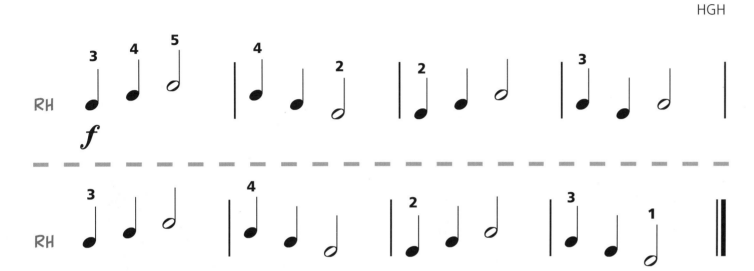

RH

f

RH

PLAYING CORNER

Also try this with the LH.
Start with the 3rd finger 8 notes lower.

Accompaniment
(Accompany an octave lower if student plays with the LH)

♩ = 108

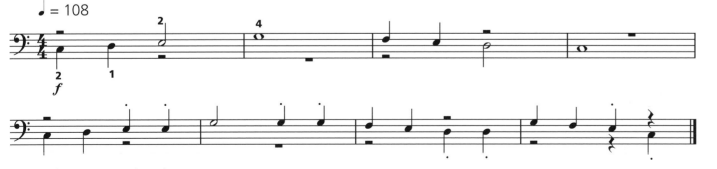

f

UNIT 6: The Stave

T1
page 20/21

➡ Notes are written on lines or in spaces:

Note on a line

Note in a space

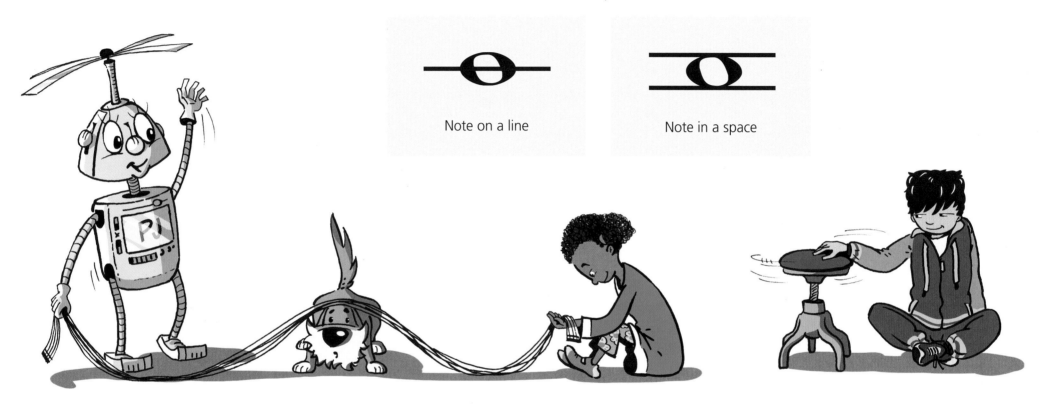

➡ Music is written on a group of 5 lines and 4 spaces. This is called a stave or staff.

lines   line notes   **spaces**   **space notes**

Up and Down

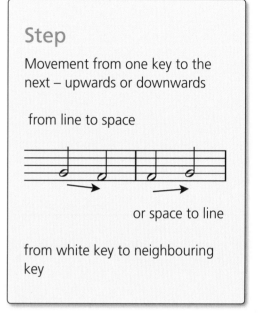

RH

MIDDLE | C D E F G | 1 2 3 4 5

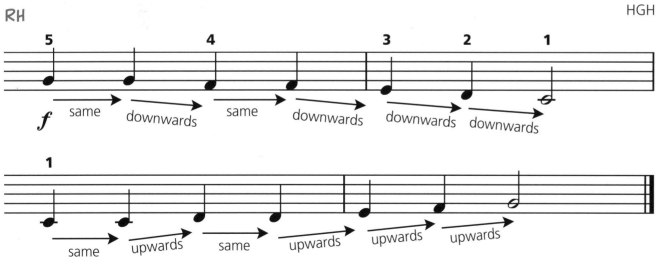

RH

HGH

5 — same — 4 — downwards — same — downwards — 3 — downwards — 2 — downwards — 1

f

1 — same — upwards — same — upwards — upwards — upwards

Step

Movement from one key to the next – upwards or downwards

from line to space

or space to line

from white key to neighbouring key

Repetition

Movement on the same key

same line — same space

same key — same key

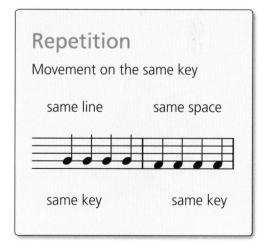

UNIT 7: Treble Clef for the Right Hand (G Clef)

T1
page 22

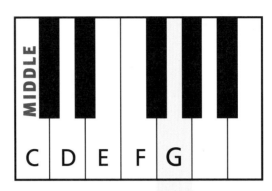

The treble clef is also called the G clef, because it circles around the G line of the stave (2nd line from the bottom).

G line

The G line in the treble clef helps you to find the other notes.

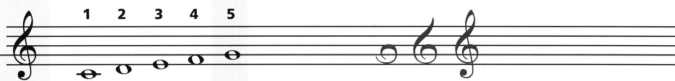

G Clef Song

HGH

G sits on the sec-ond line to help you find the notes just fine.

$\boldsymbol{f}$

Accompaniment

♩ = 80

© 2016 Schott Music Limited, London

34

▶ Audio Track **21/22**

RH

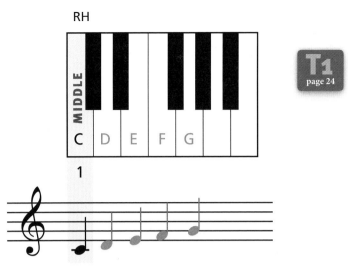

1

T1
page 24

Middle C

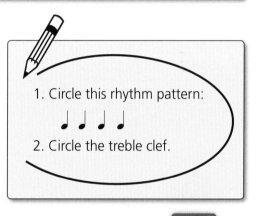

Sits on a short line known as a **leger line**

PLAYING CORNER

➡ Play the piece and count out loud.

➡ Pay attention to the correct hand and finger positions as well as to your posture.

➡ Look at the notes on the page while you are playing, not at your hands.

➡ Play the piece slowly at first. Then, try playing a little faster.

Play Middle C

D1 page 4/5 **P1** page 4 **Finger Fitness** ➤ page 70, No.1

HGH

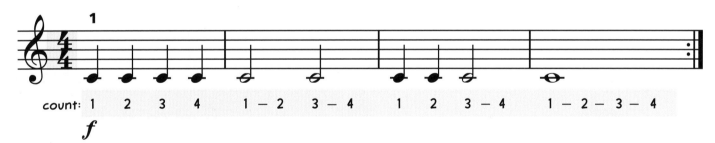

count: 1   2   3   4   1 — 2   3 — 4   1   2   3 — 4   1 — 2 — 3 — 4

f

1. Circle this rhythm pattern:

2. Circle the treble clef.

T1
page 23

4/4 Time

$\frac{4}{4}$ = **4** = 4 beats in a bar

♩ = Each beat is a crotchet

$\frac{4}{4}$ ♩ ♩ ♩ ♩ |

count: 1   2   3   4

Accompaniment

♩ = 69

f

Using Arm Weight

TECHNIQUE CORNER

Play the note C with the first finger of the RH and move your arm gently, keeping the wrist flexible. Count to 4.
Play the exercise as follows:

1 Lift the arm, upward movement of the wrist

2 Downward movement of the arm, note sounds

3 Listen to and feel the sound

4 Lift the arm, upward movement of the wrist

Exercise

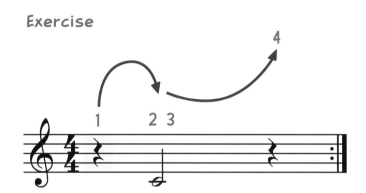

count: 1   2 – 3   4

🎵 Crotchet Rest / 🎵 Quarter Note Rest or Quarter Rest

Rest symbols represent a silence. A crotchet rest or quarter note rest lasts for one beat.

T1
page 25

Finger Movement

Exercise

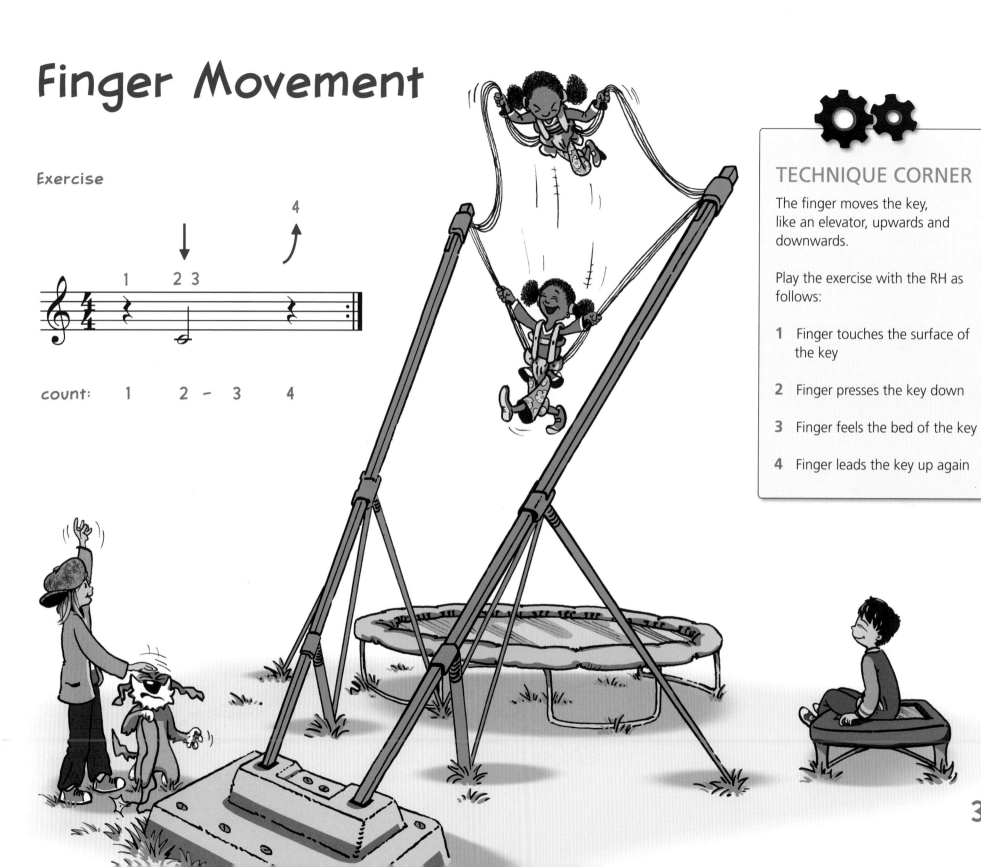

count: 1   2 - 3   4

TECHNIQUE CORNER

The finger moves the key, like an elevator, upwards and downwards.

Play the exercise with the RH as follows:

1. Finger touches the surface of the key

2. Finger presses the key down

3. Finger feels the bed of the key

4. Finger leads the key up again

The Tap Dancer

T1 page 24 **D1** page 6/7 **P1** page 5

Finger Fitness page 70, No. 2

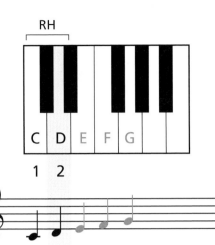

RH

C D E F G

1 2

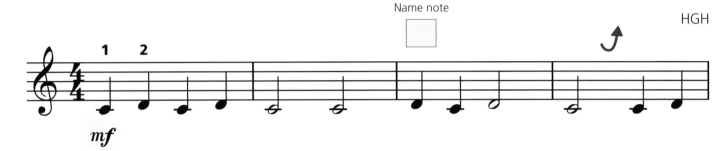

Name note

HGH

mf

mf

mezzo forte = moderately loud

5

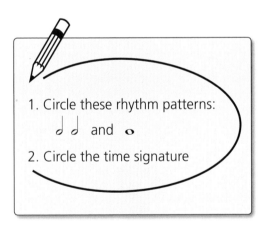

1. Circle these rhythm patterns: 𝅗𝅥 𝅗𝅥 and 𝅝

2. Circle the time signature

Accompaniment

♩ = 96

mf

© 2016 Schott Music Limited, London

Resting The Arm

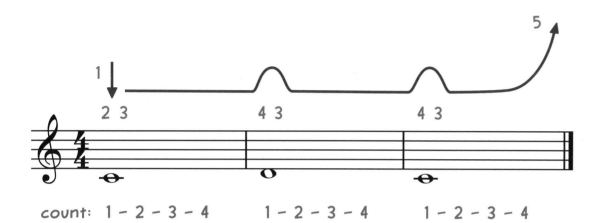

count: 1 - 2 - 3 - 4   1 - 2 - 3 - 4   1 - 2 - 3 - 4

39

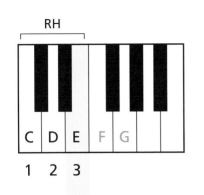

Little Waves

Finger Fitness | page 70, No. 3

mp **mezzo piano** = moderately soft

Name note

HGH

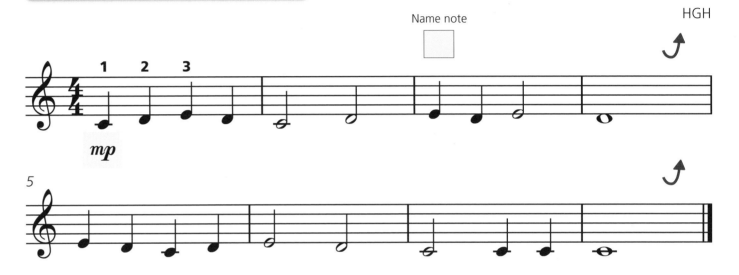

mp

5

1. Circle these rhythm patterns:

♩ ♩ ♩ and ♩ ♩ ♩

Accompaniment

♩ = 80

mp

© 2016 Schott Music Limited, London

Flash Cards

The *Flash Cards* can be used to provide further practice in note reading with musical symbols/ terms and rhythm patterns. You can collect the cards from each book.

How to use the flash cards:

1 Read the note on the card. When you are sure that you know the name of the note, you may turn the card over to check.
2 Put the cards you have read correctly on one pile, those you didn't get right on another. Keep going until you can place all the cards in the correctly-answered pile.
3 You can of course play this game with another person. For example, your piano teacher could select a card and show it to you. If you answer correctly, the card is put aside. If not, the card is mixed back in with the pack.

Flash Cards 1: Notes

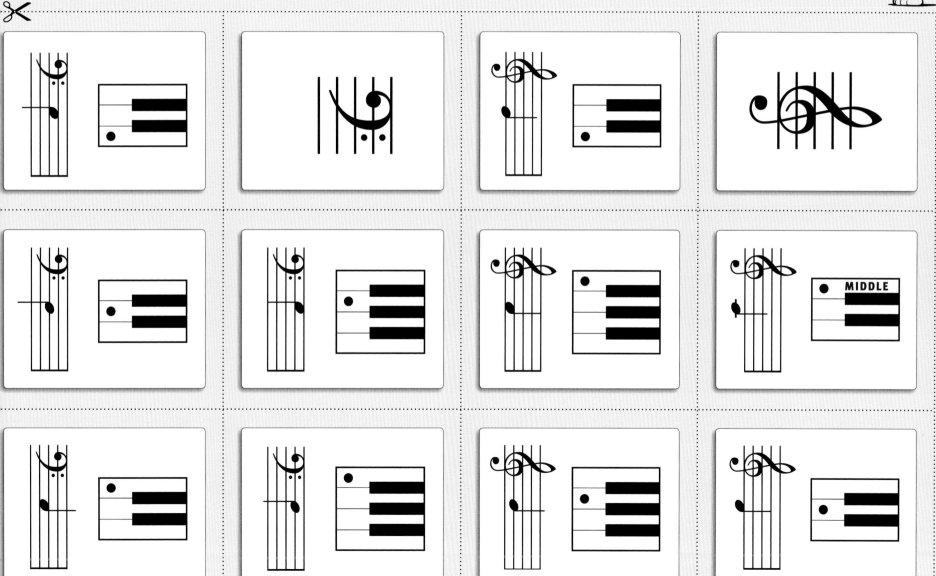

Flash Cards 1: Notes

Treble Clef or G Clef	Treble Clef E	Bass Clef or F Clef	Bass Clef E
Treble Clef C	Treble Clef F	Bass Clef G	Bass Clef D
Treble Clef D	Treble Clef G	Bass Clef F	Bass Clef C

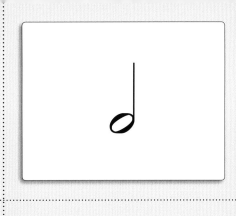

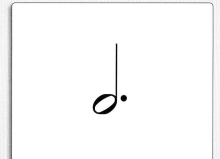

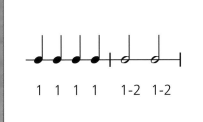

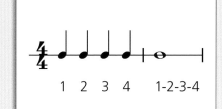

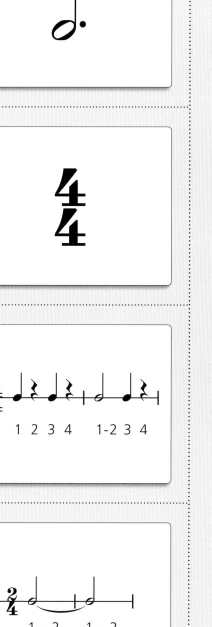

Dotted minim / half note = lasts for three beats	Semibreve / whole note = lasts for four beats	Minim / half note = lasts for two beats	Crotchet / Quarter note = lasts for one beat
Four-four time = 4 beats in a bar	Three-four time = 3 beats in a bar	Two-four time = 2 beats in a bar	Crotchet rest / Quarter note rest = lasts for one beat
Clap the rhythm and count out loud	Clap the rhythm and count out loud	Clap the rhythm and count out loud	Clap the rhythm and count out loud
Clap the rhythm and count out loud	Clap the rhythm and count out loud	Clap the rhythm and count out loud	Clap the rhythm and count out loud

p	mp	mf	f
	Andante	Moderato	Allegro
D.C. al Fine	Parallel motion	Contrary motion	Lateral motion

Repeat sign	Final bar line	Bass clef or F clef	Treble clef or G clef
forte = loud	mezzo forte = moderately loud	mezzo piano = moderately soft	piano = soft
fast	moderately fast	At a walking pace	Accent sign
One part in either hand is held, while the other part moves upwards and downwards	The parts move in opposite directions	Both hands move in the same direction	Da Capo al *Fine* = Play from the beginning until the word Fine (= end).

Spring is Coming

Finger Fitness page 70, No. 4

HGH

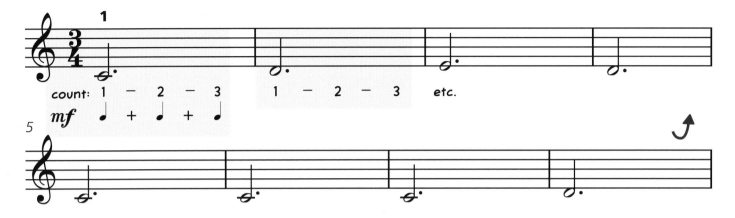

count: 1 — 2 — 3   1 — 2 — 3   etc.

mf

Accompaniment With Accompaniment, student plays one octave higher than written.

♩ = 120

mf

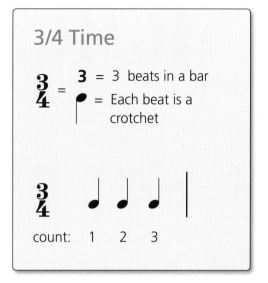

3/4 Time

$\frac{3}{4}$ = **3** = 3 beats in a bar

♩ = Each beat is a crotchet

$\frac{3}{4}$ ♩ ♩ ♩ |

count: 1 2 3

T1 page 26/27

Dotted Minim / Dotted Half Note

clear note head ↘   ← stem

♩. ← dot after the note head

count: 1 – 2 – 3
three beats

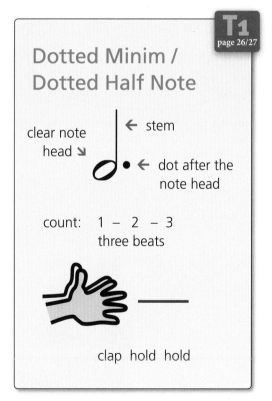

clap hold hold

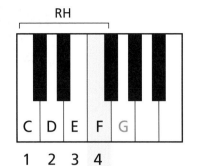

RH

C D E F G
1 2 3 4

At a Snail's Pace

T1 page 24 **P1** page 6 **Finger Fitness** page 71, No. 5

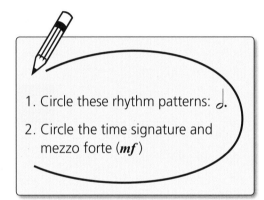

1. Circle these rhythm patterns: 𝅗𝅥.
2. Circle the time signature and mezzo forte (*mf*)

Name note

HGH

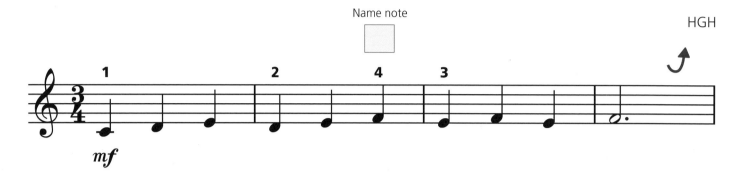

mf

Accompaniment

© 2016 Schott Music Limited, London

Piano Waltz

HGH

Accompaniment

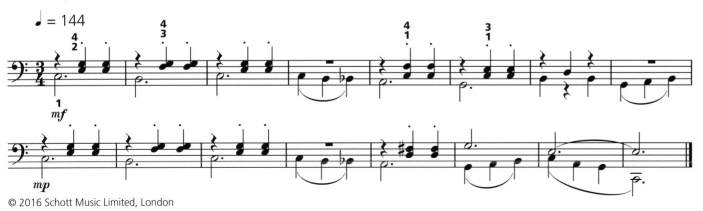

PLAYING CORNER

Try playing PIANO WALTZ with your LH. Start with the 3rd finger.

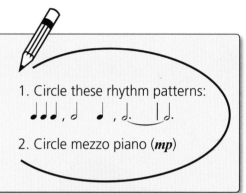

1. Circle these rhythm patterns:

2. Circle mezzo piano (**mp**)

Tie

count: 1 - 2 - 3   1 - 2 - 3

clap hold hold hold hold hold

A tie joins two notes of the same pitch with a curved line to make one long note.

Walking Along

 page 71, No. 6

German Folk Song

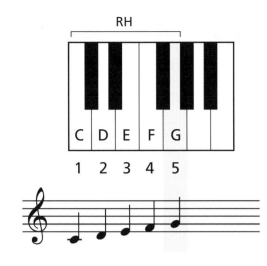

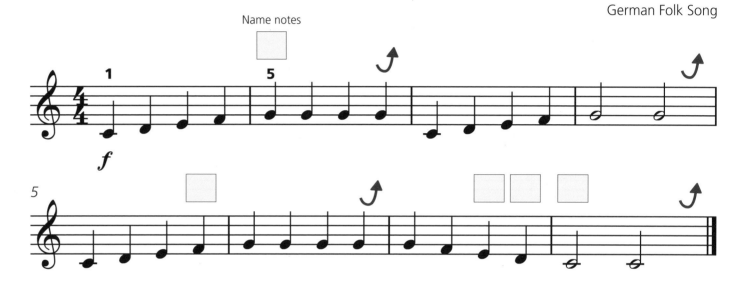

Name notes

Accompaniment

♩ = 120

Walking Along

p. 30-33

Now play it with your Left Hand

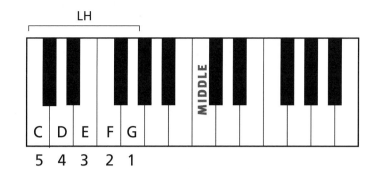

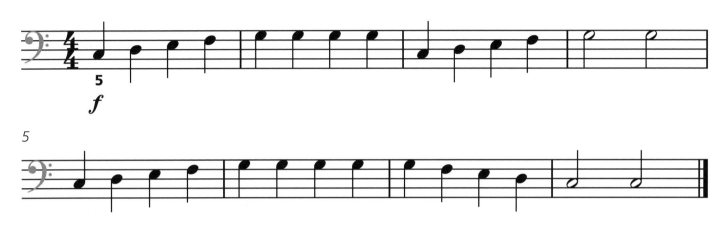

Accompaniment

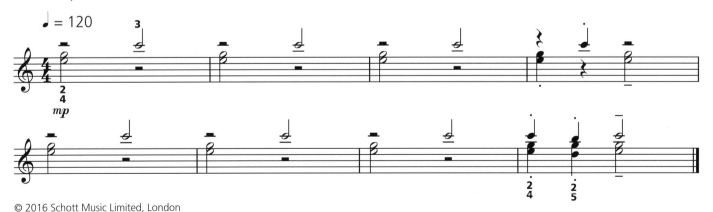

© 2016 Schott Music Limited, London

PLAYING CORNER

Try this for fun: play WALKING ALONG with the same notes, in the left hand, 8 keys lower.
If you would like to know what the clef for the LH is called, and what it looks like, turn to the next page.

UNIT 8: Bass Clef for the Left Hand (F Clef)

The F line in the bass clef helps you to find the other notes.

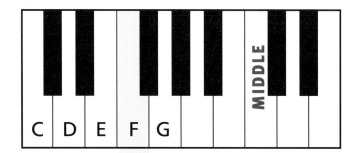

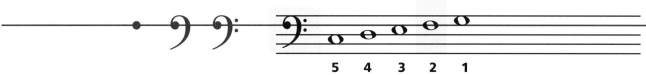

F line

The bass clef is also called the F clef, because it begins on the fourth line from the bottom and is followed by two dots.

LH

F Clef Song

HGH

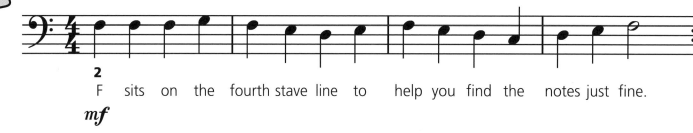

mf

F sits on the fourth stave line to help you find the notes just fine.

Accompaniment

mf

▶ Audio Track **39/40**

Oh, I See Another C

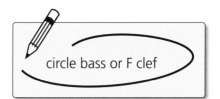

circle bass or F clef

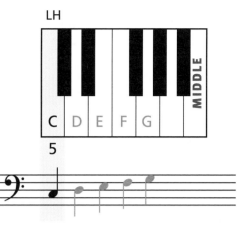

LH

C D E F G MIDDLE

5

Name note

HGH

3

mf

4

T1 page 35 D1 page 12/13 P1 page 8 ➤ Finger Fitness page 72, No. 7

PLAYING CORNER

Try playing the piece with your LH, using your 2nd finger.

Accompaniment

♩ = 60

3 5 2 1 2

mp

Dino's First Steps

T1 page 35/36 **D1** page 14/15

Finger Fitness page 72, No. 8

Name note

HGH

5
4
f

Accompaniment

♩ = 60

1. 2.

5   1

8b

f

▶ Audio Track **43/44** | Sight-Reading **7**

Frog Concert

T1 page 35/36   **D1** page 16/17   **P1** page 9

Finger Fitness   page 72, No. 9

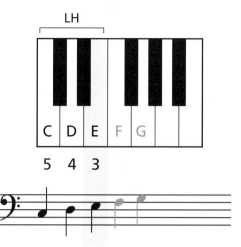

LH

C D E F G

5 4 3

Name note

HGH

mf

5

5   4   3

Accompaniment

♩ = 72

mp

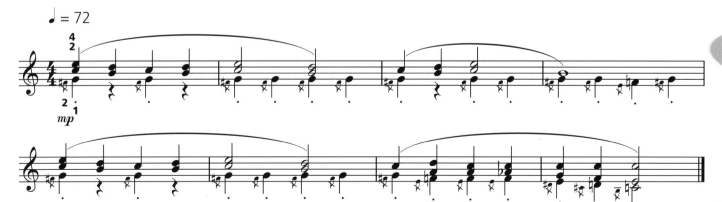

© 2016 Schott Music Limited, London

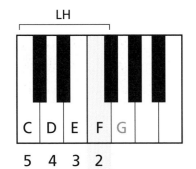

LH

Busy Bumblebee

T1 page 35/36   P1 page 10/11

Finger Fitness page 73, No. 10

Name note

HGH

Accompaniment

♩ = 132

© 2016 Schott Music Limited, London

Pirates' Melody

page 35/36

Finger Fitness page 73, No. 11

Name notes

HGH

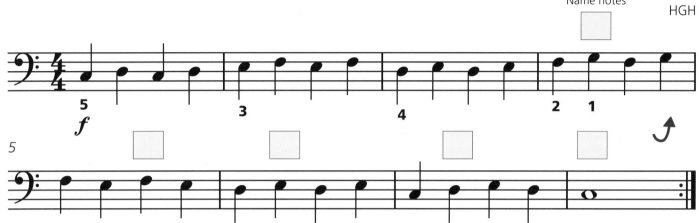

Accompaniment

♩ = 116

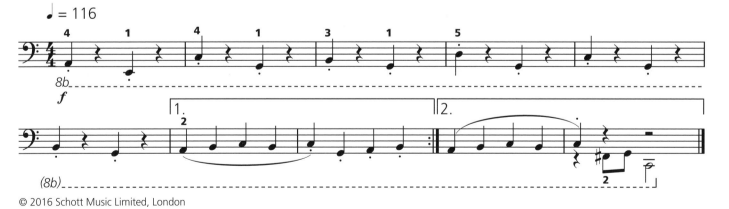

Two To Five-Note Slurs

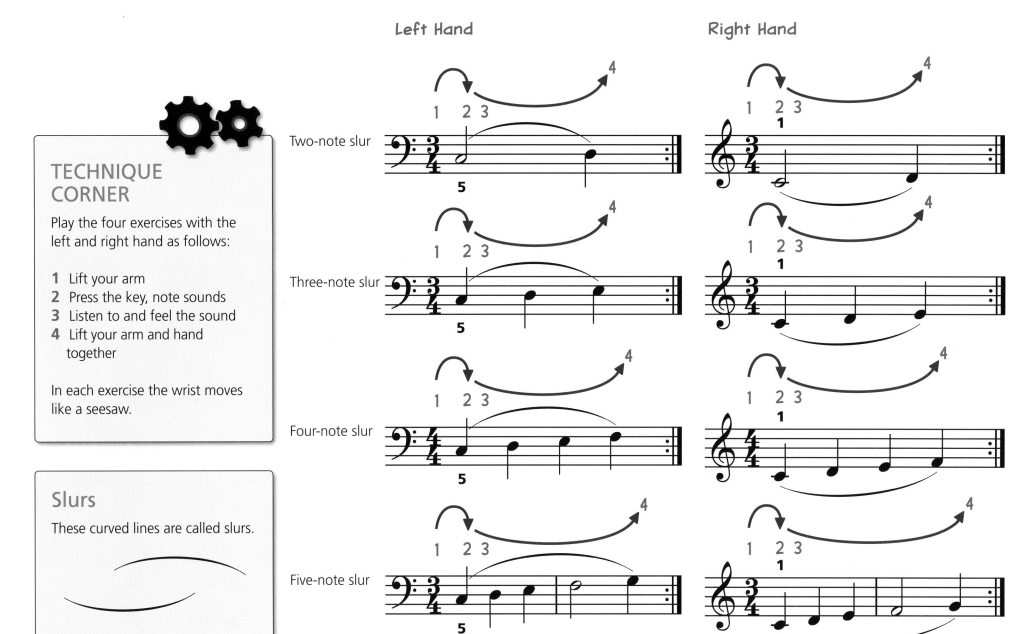

Unit 9: Reading and Writing Piano Music

C Position in Both Hands

T1 page 37

LH

RH

C D E F G   MIDDLE   C D E F G

Treble or G clef

Bracket, Brace

bar line

Bass or F clef

Stems

Up to the third line of the stave, note stems appear on the right of the note head pointing up.

Notes above the middle line have stems on the left of the note head, pointing down.

Piano music is written on two staves joined together with a bracket, or brace.

53

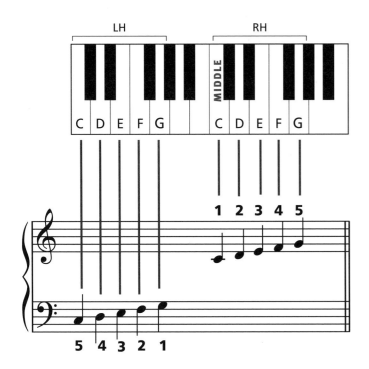

Walking Along

Melody Divided between the Hands

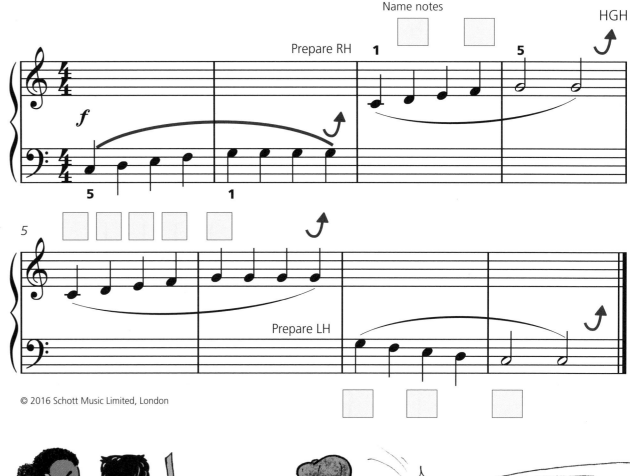

Phrases

Curved lines can also be used to group notes into musical sections or phrases.

PLAYING CORNER

Play the piece 5 notes higher. Start with G in the LH and RH.

© 2016 Schott Music Limited, London

Walking Along

 T1 page 38

With Accompaniment

HGH

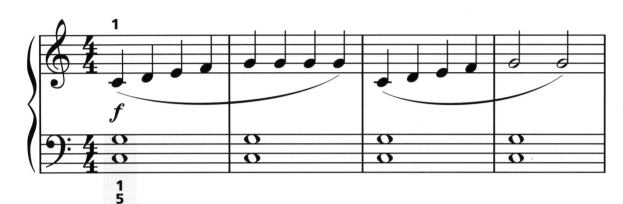

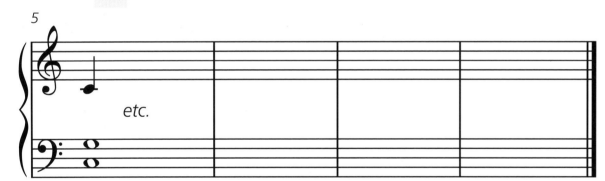

etc.

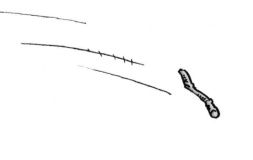

PLAYING CORNER

➡ Write down the rest of this melody.

➡ The LH accompanies each bar with two notes, one above the other, which are played at the same time. These are the lowest and highest notes in the C position. The C–G distance of 5 notes is called a *Fifth* and is also known as a *drone*.

➡ Now play the melody of WALKING ALONG in the LH and the fifth in the RH:

etc.

Fifth = Distance of 5 notes

Walking Along

  page 74, No. 12

PLAYING CORNER

➡ In the first two exercises only 4 of the 8 bars of WALKING ALONG are notated. You already know the RH melody. The LH now starts with the highest note G and plays the melody in the opposite direction at the same time. This is called **contrary motion**. Play the piece to the end.

➡ In the second exercise, both hands play the melody at the same time, in the same direction. This is called **parallel motion**. Play the piece to the end in this way.

➡ In the third exercise one hand holds the notes while the other hand moves upwards or downwards. This is called **lateral motion**.

Contrary Motion

The two hands move in opposite directions: upwards – to the right of the keyboard, and downwards – to the left of the keyboard.

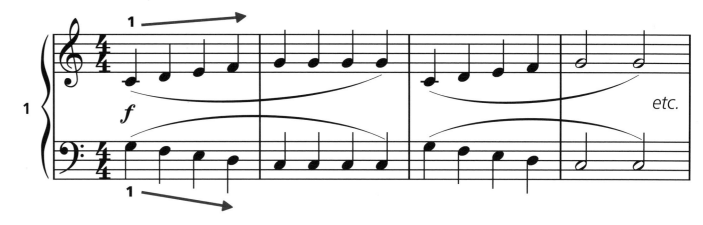

Parallel motion

Both hands move in the same direction – upwards and downwards.

 page 74, No. 13

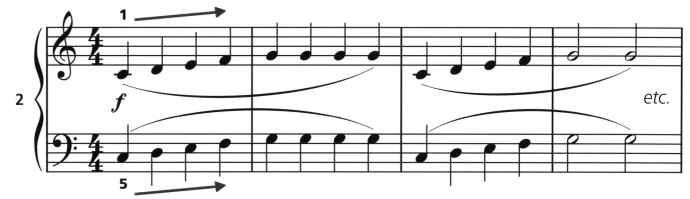

▶ Contrary Motion: Audio Track **54** | | Rhythm Check **22**
▶ Parallel Motion: Audio Track **55**

Lateral motion

One part in either hand is held, while the other part moves upwards or downwards.

Finger Fitness page 74, No. 14

T1 page 39

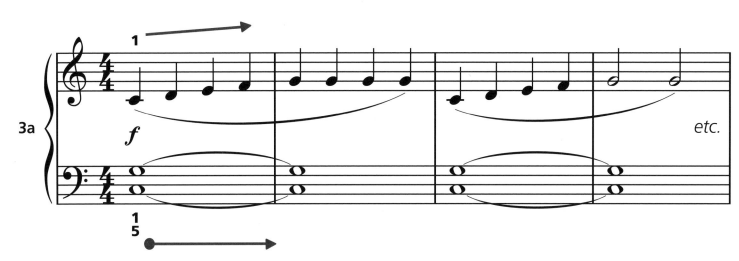

3a

f

etc.

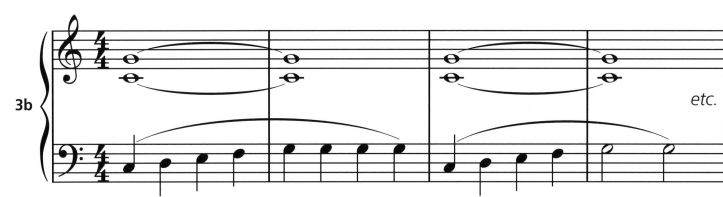

3b

etc.

© 2016 Schott Music Limited, London

PLAYING CORNER

Play the three exercises of WALKING ALONG 5 notes higher. Start with G in the RH and D in the LH.

57

Lightly Row

 **Finger Fitness** page 75, Nos.15-17

German Folk Song

Skip

Movement from one key to the next but one.

From line to line

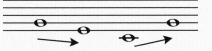

From space to space

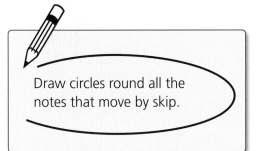

Draw circles round all the notes that move by skip.

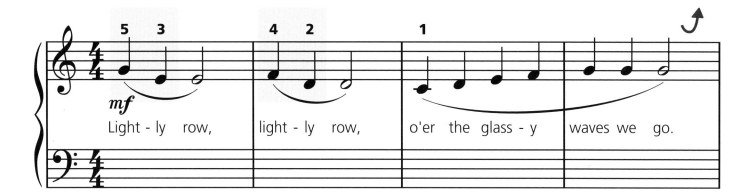

Light - ly row, light - ly row, o'er the glass - y waves we go.

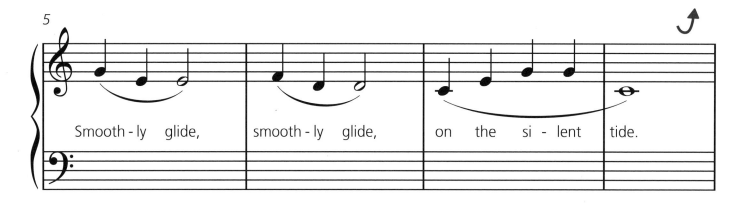

Smooth - ly glide, smooth - ly glide, on the si - lent tide.

© 2016 Schott Music Limited, London

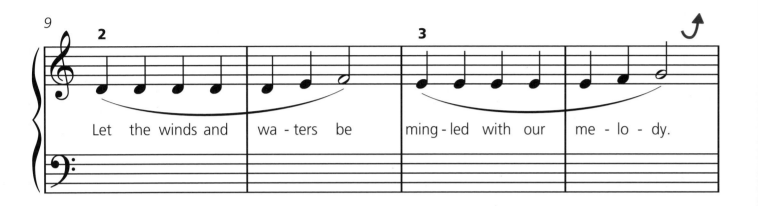

9

Let the winds and wa-ters be ming-led with our me-lo-dy.

13

Sing and float, sing and float, in our lit-tle boat.

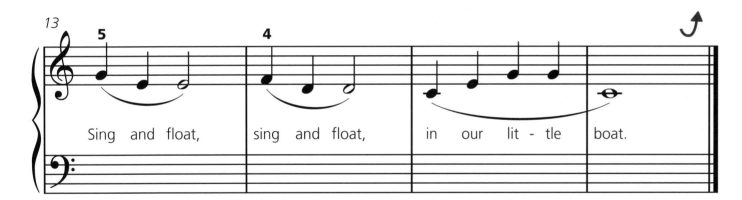

MEMORY CORNER

Play the piece from memory! Pay attention to:

➡ Repeated notes, steps and skips
➡ Fingering

Play the piece one bar at a time. Repeat each bar several times. Now link two bars, then four, and so on. You will learn the piece very quickly in this way and will easily memorize it. Now you will be able to play the piece without looking at the music.

PLAYING CORNER

➡ Now play the piece with your LH. Begin with the first finger.
➡ Try playing the piece 5 notes higher. Start with the note D.

Lightly Row

T1 page 40/41 **D1** page 24-27 **P1** page 16-19

With Accompaniment

MEMORY CORNER

The melody of LIGHTLY ROW – which you can now play from memory – is accompanied here with just two notes in the LH. These are the lowest and highest notes of the 5-finger position.

Now play the whole piece with both hands.

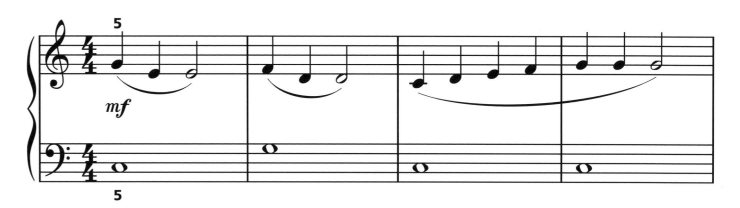

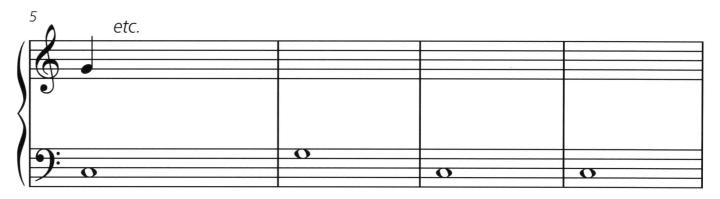

The Bagpipe Player

D1 page 28-29 **P1** page 20-23 **T1** page 42/43

PLAYING CORNER

Play the BAGPIPE PLAYER 5 notes higher in both hands. Play the piece from memory.

moderato = moderately fast

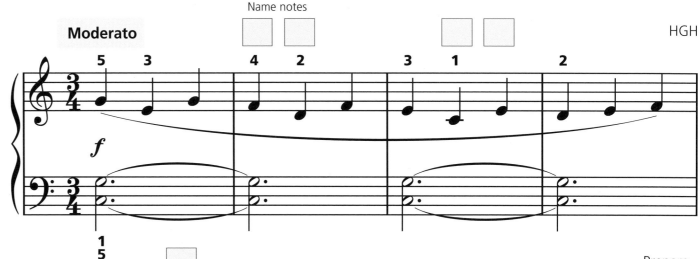

Name notes

HGH

Moderato

f

step or skip

Prepare to jump!

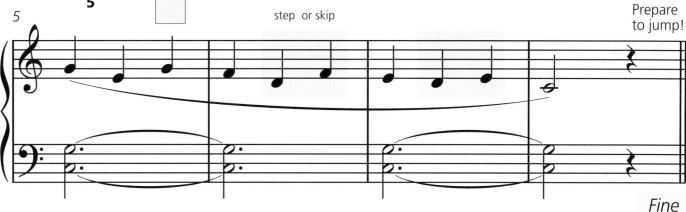

Fine

▶ Audio Track **60** | Rhythm Check **24** | Workout **10** | Sight-Reading **13**

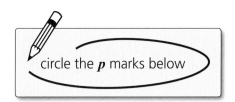
circle the **p** marks below

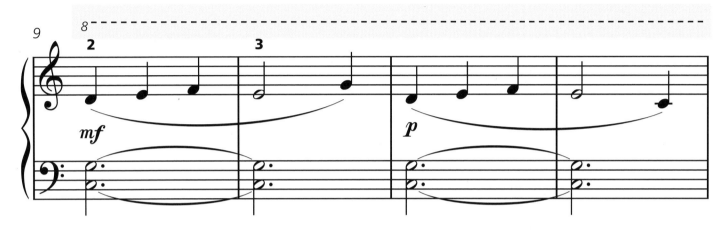

Octave Transposition Sign

8 – – – – – – ⌐

Play the notes that appear below this sign 8 notes higher than written. This applies until the end of the broken line.

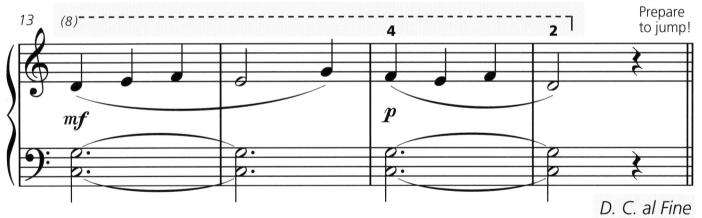

Prepare to jump!

D. C. al Fine

D. C. al Fine = Da Capo al Fine

Da Capo (= from the beginning) means go back to the beginning and play until the word **Fine** (= end).

▶ Rhythm Check **25**

63

Merrily We Roll Along

page 24-27

Finger Fitness page 76, Nos.18-19

Traditional from England
Arr.: HGH

allegro = fast

1. Circle these rhythm patterns:
♩ ♩ ♩ ♪ and ♩. ♪
2. Circle the crotchet rests

Allegro

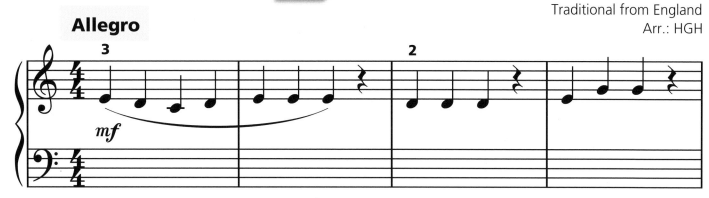

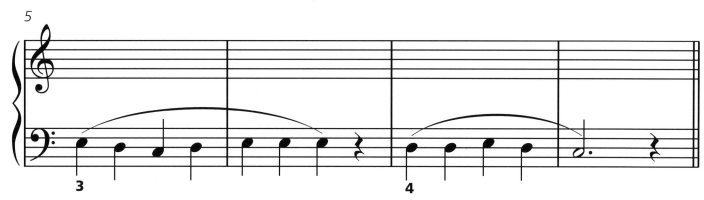

Melody in the RH and LH together

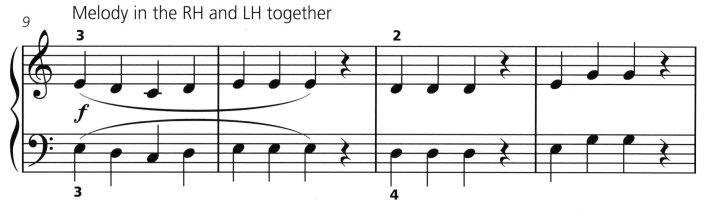

© 2016 Schott Music Limited, London

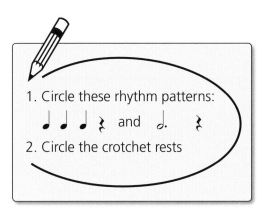

▶ Audio Track **61** | Sight-Reading **14**

13

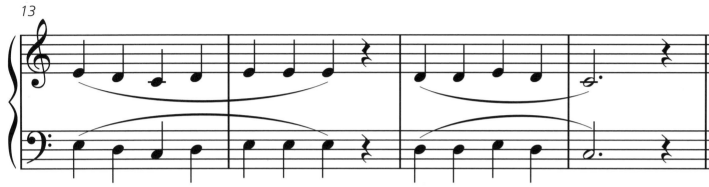

17 Melody with accompaniment

3

p

5

21

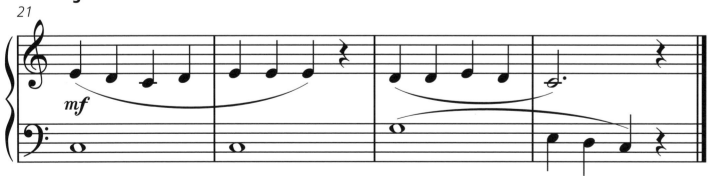

mf

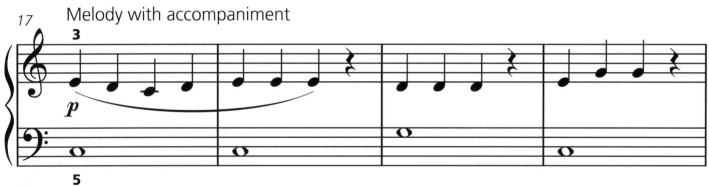

Unit 10: Playing in the 5-Finger Position with Accents

Finger Fitness page 77, No. 20

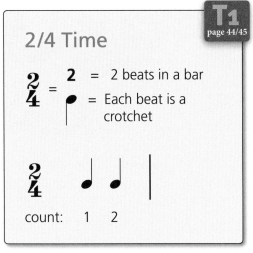

2/4 Time

T1 page 44/45

$\frac{2}{4}$ = **2** = 2 beats in a bar

= Each beat is a crotchet

$\frac{2}{4}$ ♩ ♩ |

count:　1　2

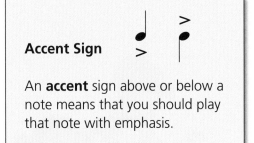

Accent Sign

An **accent** sign above or below a note means that you should play that note with emphasis.

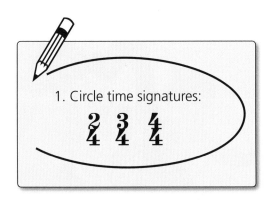

1. Circle time signatures:

$\frac{2}{4}$　$\frac{3}{4}$　$\frac{4}{4}$

HGH

Andante

Andante

P1 page 28/29

mf legato

© 2016 Schott Music Limited, London

▶ Audio Track **62** | Rhythm Check **28**　▶ Audio Track **63** | Rhythm Check **29**

Andante

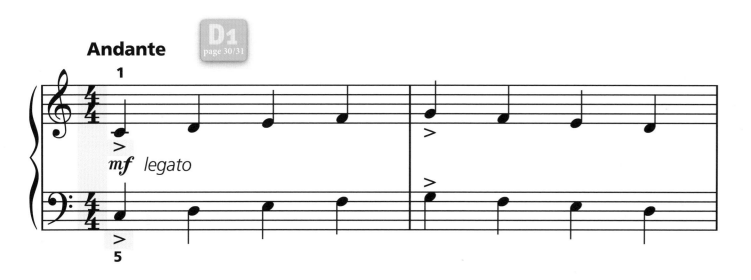

mf *legato*

© 2016 Schott Music Limited, London

TECHNIQUE CORNER

In these three exercises you play stepwise in the 5-finger position. Each exercise has a different number of beats in each bar. Emphasize the first beat of each bar.

andante = at a walking pace

▶ Audio Track **64** | Rhythm Check **30**

Piano Junior Rock

HGH

Allegro

Octave transposition sign

8 - - - - - - - ⌐

Play the note or notes that appear above this sign 8 notes lower than written.

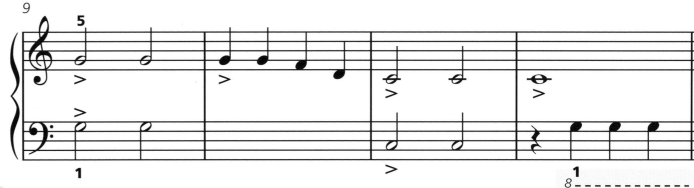

▶ Audio Track **65** | *Sight-Reading* **15**

Play the lowest C
on the piano!

69

Daily Finger Fitness 1

These are progressively graded daily finger exercises for developing finger strength and independence, evenness, accuracy and speed of playing, as well as articulation and general musicality.

Top 5 Practice Tips

➡ Make sure your hands are always in the correct position and that your posture is good.

➡ Play with each hand separately at first, then together.

➡ Practice in small sections and repeat them several times. Play the hard parts more often.

➡ With your eyes closed, imagine how your fingers move on the keyboard when playing the piece.

➡ Sing all the melodies that you play.

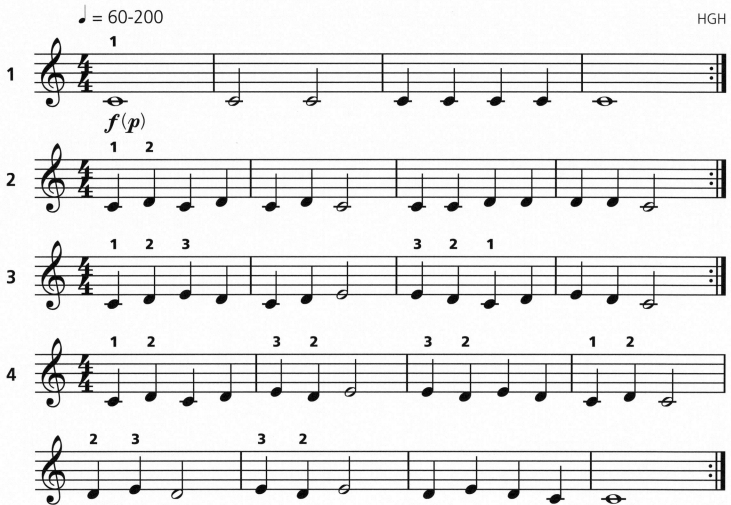

71

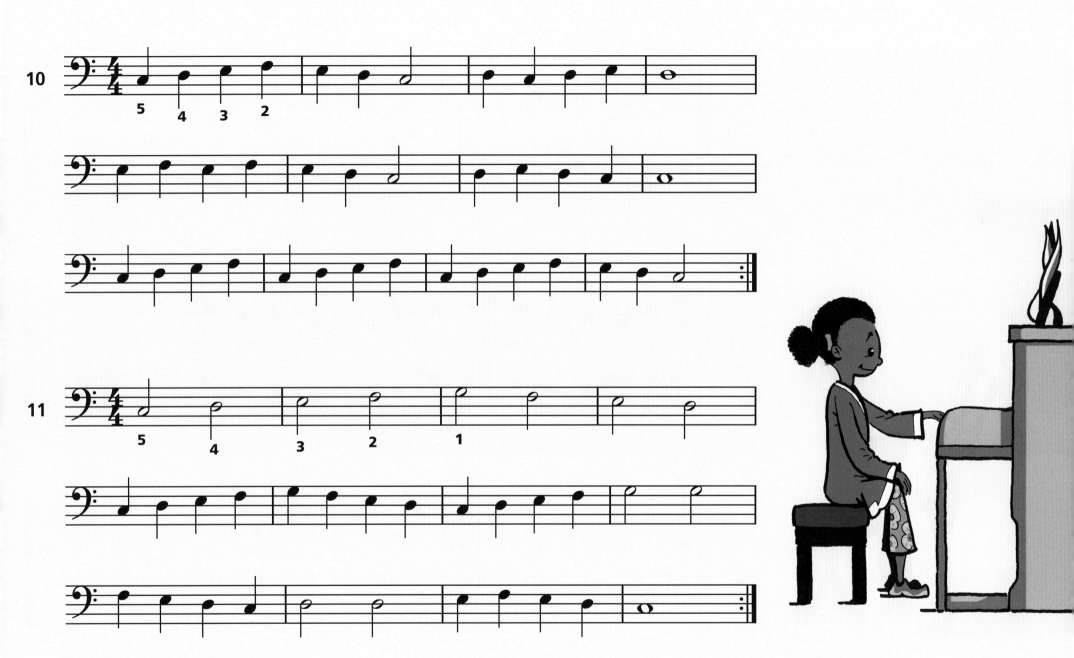

Practice first with each hand separately, then with both hands together.

74

75

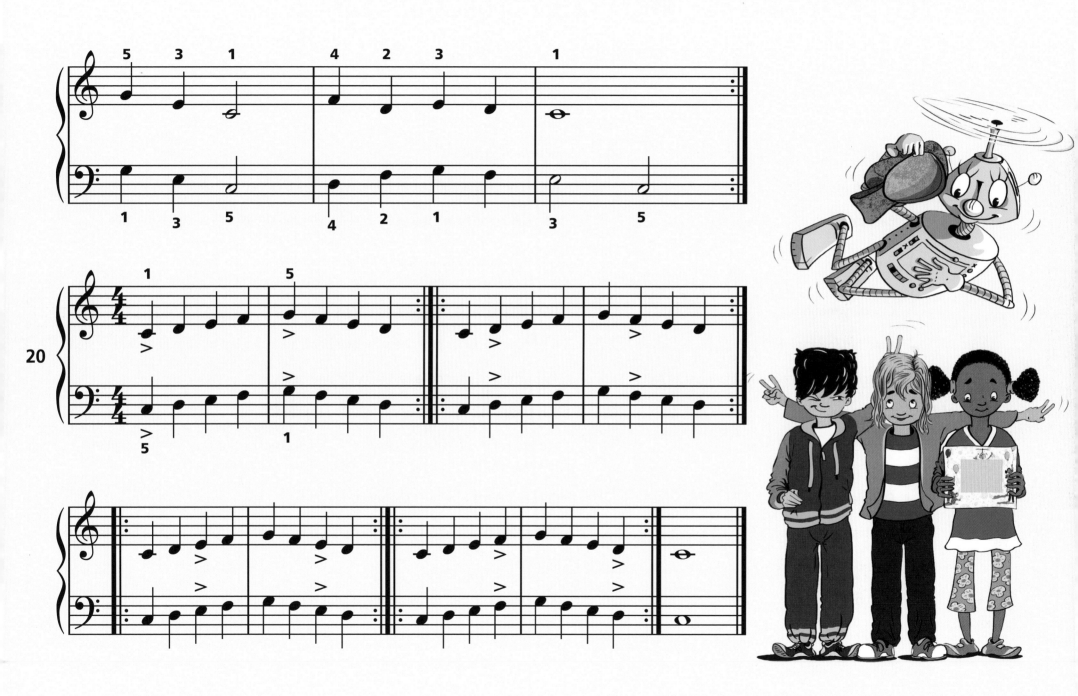

77

Important Words and Signs

>	Accent sign	Emphasize the note
	Allegro	Fast
	Andante	At a walking pace
	Bar/Measure	A bar contains a number of beats which are grouped by bar lines
𝄢	Bass clef	Also called the F clef. Notes in the bass clef are usually played with the LH
{	Bracket or Brace	This style of bracket is used to join the two staves of the piano system
	Contrary motion	The parts move in opposite directions
♩	Crotchet/quarter note	A crotchet/quarter note lasts for one beat. It has a filled-in note head with a stem
𝄽	Crotchet/quarter note rest or quarter rest	A crotchet/quarter note rest lasts for one beat
D. C. al Fine	Da Capo al Fine	Play from the beginning until the word *Fine* (end)
𝅗𝅥.	Dotted minim / half note	A dotted minim / half note lasts for three beats as the dot after a note lengthens it by half as much again. It has a clear note head followed by a dot, and a stem
‖	Double bar line	Divides a piece of music into sections
𝄂	Final bar line	At the end of a piece of music there is a normal bar line followed by a final thick bar line
f	forte	loud
𝄴 4/4	4/4 time	Four beats in a bar/measure; each beat is a crotchet
	Keyboard	The entire collection of piano keys – usually 88
	Lateral motion	One part in either hand is held, while the other part moves upwards or downwards

	legato	....	Play smoothly, without gaps between the notes
mf	mezzo forte	....	moderately loud
mp	mezzo piano	....	moderately soft
♩	Minim / half note	....	A minim / half note lasts for two beats. It has a clear note head with a stem
	Moderato	....	moderately fast
8----⌐	Octave transposition sign	....	Play the notes that appear below this sign 8 notes higher than written
⌐----8	Octave transposition sign	....	Play the notes that appear above this sign 8 notes lower than written
	Parallel motion	....	Both hands move in the same direction – upwards and downwards
	Phrase	....	A musical phrase is often indicated by a curved line or phrase mark
p	piano	....	soft
:‖	Repeat sign	....	Play again from the beginning, or repeat the section between two repeat signs
	Repetition	....	Movement on the same key
𝐨	Semibreve / whole note	....	A semibreve / whole note has a clear note head without a stem and lasts for four beats
	Skip	....	Movement from one key to the next, but one – upwards or downwards
⌒	Slurs	....	Play all notes above or beneath the slur legato
	Step	....	Movement from one key to the next – upwards or downwards
3/4	3/4 time	....	Three beats in a bar / measure; each beat is a crotchet
♩. ♩.	Tie	....	A tie joins two notes of the same pitch. The tied note is not struck again, but held for the full combined duration
𝄞	Treble clef	....	Also called the G clef. Notes in the treble clef are usually played with the RH
2/4	2/4 time	....	Two beats in a bar / measure; each beat is a crotchet

Certificate of Merit

Student _____

has successfully completed

**PIANO JUNIOR Lesson Book 1
and may now begin Book 2.**

Teacher _____

Date _____

My favourite piece was _____